Empowered Women, Empowered World

C. P. Kumar
Reiki Healer
Roorkee - 247667, India

DEDICATION

To all the women who have fought for gender equality and women's empowerment, both past and present. Your courage, determination, and resilience have paved the way for progress and inspired generations to come. This book is dedicated to you and to the ongoing pursuit of a more just and equitable world for all.

C. P. Kumar

CONTENTS

PREFACE

The empowerment of women is a critical issue that has gained increasing attention in recent years. Women have long played an essential role in society, but their contributions have often been undervalued and underappreciated. The empowerment of women is vital for achieving gender equality, creating a sustainable future, and building a better world for all.

This book, "Empowered Women, Empowered World," is a comprehensive exploration of the challenges and opportunities associated with women's empowerment. It consists of eleven chapters that cover various aspects of women's empowerment, including education, health, leadership, race and gender, entrepreneurship, politics, technology, and global best practices.

This book seeks to provide a better understanding of what women's empowerment means, why it is necessary, and how it can be achieved. Each chapter is designed to highlight a specific area where women's empowerment is crucial, providing insights into the challenges and opportunities that women face and offering strategies for promoting gender equality.

The book is intended to be a valuable resource for policymakers, activists, researchers, educators, and anyone interested in contributing to the cause of gender equality. It is our hope that this book will inspire readers to take action to empower women, promote gender equality, and create a more just and equitable world.

C. P. Kumar
Reiki Healer

Chapter 1. Understanding Women's Empowerment
Definition, Challenges, and Opportunities

Introduction

Women's empowerment is a complex concept that has gained significant attention in recent years. It involves a wide range of factors that contribute to women's ability to achieve equality and autonomy in various aspects of their lives. In this article, we will explore the definition, challenges, and opportunities related to women's empowerment.

What is Women's Empowerment?

Women's empowerment refers to the process of enabling women to have control over their lives and achieve their full potential. This can include various aspects of life such as economic, political, social, and personal development. Women's empowerment aims to address gender inequalities and promote women's rights, agency, and participation in decision-making processes.

Challenges to Women's Empowerment

Despite the growing attention and efforts towards women's empowerment, there are still several challenges that hinder progress in this area. Some of the significant challenges include:

1. Gender-based violence: Women continue to experience different forms of violence, including sexual, physical, emotional, and psychological abuse. This violence undermines women's autonomy and ability to participate fully in society.

2. Economic Inequality: Women are still paid less than men for similar work, have limited access to finance, and are often confined to low-paying jobs. This economic inequality limits their ability to achieve their full potential and participate fully in economic activities.

3. Limited political representation: Women are underrepresented in political positions globally. This lack of representation denies them the opportunity to participate in

decision-making processes, which affects policies that directly affect them.

4. Societal and cultural barriers: Societal and cultural beliefs and norms continue to limit women's access to education, healthcare, and other basic rights. This limits their ability to achieve their full potential and participate fully in society.

Opportunities for Women's Empowerment

Despite the challenges, there are several opportunities for women's empowerment that have emerged in recent years. These opportunities include:

1. Education: Education is one of the critical drivers of women's empowerment. Access to education opens up opportunities for women to acquire knowledge and skills, which can help them participate fully in society.

2. Economic Empowerment: Economic empowerment initiatives, such as microfinance and entrepreneurship programs, have the potential to increase women's income and access to finance,

allowing them to become economically independent.

3. Policy and Legislative reforms: Governments can enact policies and legislation that promote gender equality and empower women. These policies can include measures such as quotas for women's representation in political positions and equal pay for equal work.

4. Technology: Technology has the potential to bridge the gender gap and create opportunities for women's empowerment. Initiatives such as digital literacy programs, online education, and telecommuting can help women access information and opportunities, regardless of their location.

Conclusion

Women's empowerment is a critical component of achieving gender equality and promoting sustainable development. While there are several challenges to women's empowerment, there are also opportunities that can be leveraged to drive progress in this area. It is essential to continue investing in initiatives that promote women's rights, agency, and participation in decision-making processes to achieve lasting change.

How Education Can Empower Women and Change the World

Introduction

Education is a powerful tool that can empower women and change the world. It has been shown time and again that education is one of the most effective ways to improve the lives of women and promote gender equality. In this article, we will explore the power of education and how it can help to empower women and create a better future for all.

Education is a fundamental human right, and it is essential for the social, economic, and political development of individuals and societies. However, for many women around the world, access to education is limited or nonexistent. According to UNESCO, there are still 132 million girls worldwide who are out of school. This lack of access to education has a significant impact on women and their ability to lead fulfilling lives.

Education and Empowerment

Education is a key factor in empowering women. It provides them with the knowledge and skills they need to participate fully in their communities and societies. Education helps women to gain a sense of self-worth and confidence, and it enables them to make informed decisions about their lives.

Empowered women are better able to advocate for their rights, participate in decision-making processes, and challenge gender-based discrimination and stereotypes. They are also more likely to have access to economic opportunities and to be able to improve their own lives and those of their families.

Education and Health

Education has a significant impact on women's health. Educated women are more likely to have access to healthcare, and they are better able to take care of themselves and their families. They are also more likely to have healthy pregnancies and to give birth to healthy babies.

In addition, education can help to improve the health of communities as a whole. Educated women are better equipped to educate others about health issues and to promote healthy behaviors. They are also more likely to be involved in community health programs and to advocate for better healthcare services.

Education and Economic Empowerment

Education is a critical factor in economic empowerment. It provides women with the skills and knowledge they need to participate in the labor market and to earn a living. Educated women are more likely to have access to formal employment, and they are also more likely to start their own businesses.

In addition, education can help to break the cycle of poverty. Educated women are better able to provide for their families, and they are also more likely to invest in their children's education. This, in turn, can lead to better outcomes for future generations.

Education and Political Empowerment

Education is also a key factor in political empowerment. It provides women with the knowledge and skills they need to participate fully in political processes and to advocate for their rights. Educated women are more likely to be involved in politics, and they are also more likely to hold positions of power and influence.

In addition, education can help to challenge gender-based discrimination and stereotypes in politics. Educated women are better able to challenge the status quo and to advocate for policies that promote gender equality.

Challenges to Women's Education

Despite the many benefits of education, there are still many challenges that prevent women from accessing education. These challenges include poverty, cultural barriers, discrimination, and conflict and instability.

Poverty is one of the main barriers to education for women. Many families cannot afford to send their daughters to school, and girls are often expected to help with household chores or to work outside the home. In addition, cultural barriers can prevent girls from attending school, especially in conservative societies where girls are expected to stay at home and take care of the household.

Discrimination is also a significant barrier to women's education. Girls and women may face discrimination based on their gender, ethnicity, religion, or social status. This discrimination can take many forms, including harassment, Conflict and instability can also have a significant impact on women's education. In areas affected by conflict or natural disasters, schools may be destroyed, and teachers may flee. This can make it difficult or impossible for girls to attend school, and it can also increase the risk of violence and exploitation.

Overcoming these challenges requires a coordinated effort from governments, civil society, and the international community. It is essential to address the root causes of poverty, discrimination, and conflict and to provide girls with the support they need to access and complete their education.

Conclusion

Education is a powerful tool that can empower women and change the world. It is essential for women's health, economic empowerment, political empowerment, and overall well-being. Educated women are better able to advocate for their rights, participate in decision-making processes, and challenge gender-based discrimination and stereotypes.

However, there are still many challenges that prevent women from accessing education. Poverty, cultural barriers, discrimination, and conflict and instability all contribute to the problem. It is essential to address these challenges and to provide girls with the support they need to access and complete their education.

Investing in women's education is not only the right thing to do; it is also the smart thing to do. Educated women can help to break the cycle of poverty, promote gender equality, and create a better future for all. By empowering women through education, we can change the world for the better.

Introduction

Women's health and empowerment are closely intertwined, and achieving equality requires breaking down the various barriers that stand in the way of progress. Women around the world face a range of challenges that impact their health and well-being, from gender-based violence to limited access to healthcare and education. However, progress is being made, and there are numerous initiatives and movements aimed at advancing the cause of women's health and empowerment. In this article, we'll take a closer look at some of the key issues and strategies involved in breaking down barriers and achieving equality for women.

The Importance of Women's Health

Women's health is a fundamental component of overall public health, and yet women often face significant challenges when it comes to accessing healthcare services. In many parts of the world, women may not have access to basic healthcare services like reproductive care, prenatal care, or mental health services. This can lead to serious health problems and complications that can impact women's quality of life and even put their lives at risk.

One major issue that impacts women's health is the lack of education around sexual and reproductive health. Many girls and women are not taught about their bodies, sexual health, or contraception, which can lead to unintended pregnancies and other health complications. This lack of education can also contribute to the spread of sexually transmitted infections and other health problems.

Gender-Based Violence

Gender-based violence is a significant barrier to women's health and empowerment. This includes physical, sexual, and emotional abuse, as well as harassment and discrimination. These types of violence can have a profound impact on women's mental and physical health, and can also limit their opportunities and ability to participate in society.

In recent years, there has been growing recognition of the need to address gender-based violence and protect women's rights. This has led to the development of laws and policies aimed at preventing violence against women, as well as initiatives to support survivors and promote gender equality.

Access to Education and Employment

Access to education and employment is another key factor in women's health and empowerment. Education is essential for empowering women to make informed choices about their health and well-being, as well as for improving economic opportunities and social mobility. However, in many parts of the world, girls and women may not have access to education, or they may face discrimination and bias in the classroom and workplace.

Employment is also critical for women's empowerment, as it provides economic independence and can help to break the cycle of poverty. However, women often face discrimination and unequal pay in the workplace, which can limit their opportunities for career advancement and financial stability.

Strategies for Empowerment

There are numerous strategies that can be employed to promote women's health and empowerment. These include:

1. Education: Providing education and resources to girls and women is essential for empowering them to make informed decisions about their health and well-being. This includes education around sexual and reproductive health, as well as access to resources like contraception and healthcare services.

2. Economic empowerment: Providing women with access to employment and economic opportunities can help to promote their independence and improve their quality of life. This includes initiatives like microfinance programs, vocational training, and policies aimed at reducing gender discrimination in the workplace.

3. Laws and policies: Laws and policies aimed at promoting gender equality and protecting women's rights are essential for

breaking down barriers and achieving equality. This includes laws against gender-based violence, policies promoting equal pay and equal opportunities in the workplace, and initiatives aimed at promoting women's political participation.

4. Community engagement: Engaging communities in efforts to promote women's health and empowerment can help to build support and promote lasting change. This includes initiatives like community-based health programs, advocacy campaigns, and efforts to promote women's leadership and participation in decision-making.

Conclusion

Women's health and empowerment are critical components of overall public health and social well-being. Achieving equality for women requires breaking down the various barriers that stand in the way of progress, including gender-based violence, limited access to healthcare and education, and discrimination in the workplace. There are numerous strategies that can be employed to promote women's health and empowerment, including education, economic empowerment, laws and policies, and community engagement.

Progress has been made in recent years, but there is still much work to be done. It is essential that we continue to support initiatives and movements aimed at breaking down barriers and achieving equality for women. By working together, we can create a world where all women have access to the resources and opportunities they need to thrive.

Ultimately, the goal of promoting women's health and empowerment is not just about achieving gender equality, but about building a better, more equitable world for all people. When women are healthy and empowered, they are better able to contribute to their families, communities, and societies, and the benefits of this empowerment are felt by everyone. By breaking down barriers and promoting women's health and empowerment, we can build a brighter future for all.

Introduction

Women have made significant progress in recent years, breaking down barriers and shattering stereotypes. However, there is still a long way to go when it comes to achieving gender equality, particularly in leadership roles. Despite the progress that has been made, women continue to face significant obstacles and challenges in their pursuit of leadership positions. In this article, we will explore these obstacles and discuss strategies that women can use to overcome them and achieve success in leadership roles.

Obstacles Faced by Women in Leadership

The obstacles faced by women in leadership are varied and complex. Some of the most significant include:

1. Gender Bias: One of the most significant obstacles that women face is gender bias. This can take many forms, including assumptions about women's abilities and leadership styles, as well as outright discrimination.

2. Lack of Representation: Another challenge faced by women is the lack of representation in leadership positions. Women are still underrepresented in many industries and sectors, which can make it difficult for them to break into leadership roles.

3. Stereotyping: Stereotyping is another obstacle that women face, with many people assuming that women are not cut out for leadership positions or that they are too emotional or too nurturing to be effective leaders.

4. Work-Life Balance: Women are often expected to balance their leadership roles with family responsibilities, which can be challenging and require significant sacrifice.

5. Impostor Syndrome: Impostor syndrome is a psychological phenomenon where individuals doubt their abilities and accomplishments and feel like frauds. This

can be particularly common among women in leadership roles who may feel like they do not belong or are not qualified.

Strategies for Overcoming Obstacles

While the obstacles faced by women in leadership can be daunting, there are strategies that women can use to overcome them and achieve success. Some of these strategies include:

1. Building a Support Network: Building a support network of mentors, colleagues, and friends can be incredibly beneficial for women in leadership. These individuals can provide advice, support, and encouragement, helping women navigate the challenges they face.

2. Developing a Strong Personal Brand: Developing a strong personal brand can help women establish their credibility and demonstrate their expertise. This can be particularly important for women who may be facing gender bias or stereotyping.

3. Seeking Out Leadership Opportunities: Seeking out leadership opportunities, even if

they are outside of one's comfort zone, can help women build their skills and demonstrate their leadership abilities.

4. Advocating for Yourself: **Women in leadership roles need to be able to advocate for themselves, particularly when it comes to compensation and promotion opportunities. This can involve negotiating for better pay, asking for promotions, and speaking up when they feel their contributions are not being recognized.**

5. Embracing Failure: **Failure is an inevitable part of any leadership journey, and women need to learn to embrace it and use it as a learning opportunity. By reframing failure as an opportunity for growth, women can develop resilience and perseverance, which are critical traits for successful leaders.**

6. Challenging Gender Bias: **Challenging gender bias can be a powerful way for women to overcome obstacles and achieve success. This can involve calling out biased behaviors or language, advocating for diversity and inclusion initiatives, and mentoring other women to help them achieve their leadership goals.**

Success Stories of Women in Leadership

Despite the challenges they face, many women have achieved incredible success in leadership roles. Here are just a few examples:

1. Mary Barra: Mary Barra is the CEO of General Motors, making her the first woman to lead a major global automaker. Under her leadership, GM has undergone significant changes, including a shift towards electric and autonomous vehicles.

2. Sheryl Sandberg: Sheryl Sandberg is the COO of Facebook and the author of the best-selling book Lean In. Sandberg has been a vocal advocate for women in the workplace, encouraging them to pursue leadership roles and challenge gender stereotypes.

3. Ursula von der Leyen: Ursula von der Leyen is the President of the European Commission, making her the first woman to hold this position. She has been a vocal advocate for gender equality, and under her leadership, the European Union has

launched initiatives to promote gender equality and combat gender-based violence.

4. Ginni Rometty: Ginni Rometty is the former CEO of IBM, making her the first woman to lead the company. She is also a strong advocate for diversity and inclusion in the workplace, and under her leadership, IBM launched a range of initiatives to promote gender and racial equality.

5. Jacinda Ardern: Jacinda Ardern has been the Prime Minister of New Zealand, making her the country's third female leader. Ardern has been widely praised for her leadership during the COVID-19 pandemic, and she is also known for her focus on social justice issues, including gender equality and climate change.

These women, and many others like them, have shattered glass ceilings and broken down barriers, paving the way for future generations of women leaders.

Conclusion

Women in leadership face significant obstacles, including gender bias, lack of representation, stereotyping, work-life balance, and impostor syndrome. However, there are strategies that women can use to overcome these obstacles and achieve success, including building a support network, developing a strong personal brand, seeking out leadership opportunities, advocating for oneself, embracing failure, and challenging gender bias. By using these strategies and learning from the success stories of other women leaders, women can continue to break down barriers and make progress towards achieving true gender equality in leadership roles.

Introduction

Empowerment is a multifaceted concept that encompasses a range of social, psychological, and economic factors. While empowerment can be experienced by anyone, women of color face unique challenges when it comes to achieving and maintaining a sense of empowerment. The intersection of race, gender, and empowerment can be a complex and nuanced topic, and it is important to explore the experiences of women of color in order to better understand the barriers they face and how they can be overcome.

The Role of Intersectionality in Empowerment

Intersectionality is a concept that was first introduced by legal scholar Kimberlé Crenshaw in 1989. It describes the interconnected nature of social identities, such as race, gender, class, and sexuality, and how these identities intersect to create unique experiences of oppression and privilege. Intersectionality is particularly relevant to the study of women of color and empowerment because it highlights the ways in which these women face multiple layers of discrimination that can impact their ability to achieve empowerment.

Racial and Gender Discrimination

One of the primary challenges that women of color face when it comes to empowerment is racial and gender discrimination. Women of color may experience discrimination in a variety of settings, from the workplace to the healthcare system to the criminal justice system. Discrimination can take many forms, including overt acts of prejudice, microaggressions, and implicit bias.

For example, women of color may be passed over for job opportunities or promotions because of their race or gender, despite their qualifications. They may also be subjected to higher levels of scrutiny or criticism than their white or male colleagues. In healthcare settings, women of color may be less likely to receive adequate care due to racial and gender biases on the part of medical professionals. And in the criminal justice system, women of color may be disproportionately targeted and punished due to racial biases and stereotypes.

All of these forms of discrimination can contribute to a sense of disempowerment among women of color. When they are constantly told that they are not as valuable or deserving as others, it can be difficult to feel empowered and confident in their abilities.

Economic Inequality

Another factor that can impact the empowerment of women of color is economic inequality. Women of color are more likely to live in poverty and to experience financial insecurity than their white counterparts. This can be due to a variety of factors, including discrimination in the workplace, lack of access to education and training, and systemic barriers to wealth accumulation.

Economic inequality can have a significant impact on a woman's sense of empowerment. When she is struggling to make ends meet, it can be difficult to focus on personal growth and development. She may be too busy working multiple jobs or taking care of her family to invest time and energy in activities that could help her achieve her goals.

Cultural Factors

Cultural factors can also play a role in the empowerment of women of color. For example, some cultural norms may place greater emphasis on collectivism rather than individualism. While this can be a positive value in many ways, it can also make it difficult for women to prioritize their own needs and goals. They may feel pressure to prioritize their family or community over their own personal growth and development.

Similarly, cultural norms around femininity and masculinity can impact how women of color are perceived and treated. For example, Black women may be seen as "strong" and "resilient," which can be positive attributes in many ways. However, these same attributes can also be used to justify expectations that Black women should be able to handle more stress or adversity than their white counterparts. This can make it difficult for Black women to ask for help or to prioritize self-care.

Strategies for Empowerment

Despite the challenges that women of color face when it comes to empowerment, there are a variety of strategies that can help them achieve and maintain empowerment. Here are a few examples:

1. Building Support Networks

Building supportive relationships with other women of color can be an important strategy for empowerment. When women can connect with others who have shared experiences, they may feel less isolated and more validated. These relationships can provide emotional support and help women to see themselves as part of a larger community of strong and capable women.

2. Pursuing Education and Training

Access to education and training can be a powerful tool for empowerment. When women of color have the opportunity to develop new skills and knowledge, they may feel more confident and capable. Education can also open up new career opportunities and increase earning potential, which can help to address economic inequality.

3. Advocating for Change

Advocacy can be an important strategy for women of color who want to see change in their communities and society at large. This can involve speaking out about issues that impact them personally, supporting policies and programs that promote equality and justice, and working to create more inclusive and welcoming environments.

4. Prioritizing Self-Care

Self-care is an important component of empowerment. When women take care of themselves, they may feel more energized and better able to tackle challenges. This can involve a variety of activities, from exercise and healthy eating to therapy and meditation.

Conclusion

Empowerment is a crucial aspect of individual and societal well-being. However, achieving and maintaining a sense of empowerment can be particularly challenging for women of color due to the intersection of race, gender, and other social identities. By understanding the unique challenges faced by women of color, we can work to create more inclusive and equitable environments that support their growth and success. Through building supportive networks, pursuing education and training, advocating for change, and prioritizing self-care, women of color can overcome barriers to empowerment and achieve their goals.

Introduction

Despite significant progress made over the years, women still face significant challenges in the workplace. They continue to be underrepresented in leadership positions, earn less than their male counterparts, and often face discrimination, harassment, and other barriers that hinder their professional growth and advancement. Achieving gender parity in the workplace is not only a matter of fairness and social justice, but it is also critical for driving innovation, productivity, and sustainable economic growth. In this article, we explore some of the strategies that can be employed to empower women in the workplace and help them overcome the obstacles that hold them back.

Promoting Gender Diversity

One of the most critical strategies for empowering women in the workplace is promoting gender diversity. It is essential to have more women in leadership positions to provide role models and mentors to other women, break down stereotypes, and challenge unconscious biases. Organizations can achieve gender diversity by setting targets, developing strategies to attract and retain female talent, and implementing inclusive policies and practices. Some of the initiatives that organizations can adopt include:

- ❖ Establishing diversity and inclusion committees or task forces
- ❖ Providing unconscious bias training to hiring managers and supervisors
- ❖ Conducting gender pay equity analyses and taking corrective actions
- ❖ Implementing flexible work arrangements such as telecommuting, job sharing, and flexible schedules
- ❖ Offering maternity and paternity leave and other family-friendly policies

- ❖ Providing mentoring and coaching programs for women
- ❖ Developing career development programs and leadership training for women

Addressing Bias and Stereotypes

Another critical strategy for empowering women in the workplace is addressing bias and stereotypes. Gender bias can manifest in various forms, including unconscious biases, microaggressions, and discrimination. These biases can hinder women's career advancement, limit their opportunities, and contribute to a hostile work environment. Some of the ways to address bias and stereotypes include:

- Encouraging open and honest communication about diversity and inclusion
- Holding managers and supervisors accountable for creating an inclusive workplace
- Providing training and resources to address unconscious biases and stereotypes

- Encouraging women to speak up and report discrimination, harassment, or other forms of bias
- Developing policies and procedures that promote fairness and equality
- Using diverse hiring panels and ensuring job descriptions are gender-neutral

Creating a Supportive Workplace Culture

Creating a supportive workplace culture is critical for empowering women in the workplace. Women who feel supported and valued are more likely to stay with their current employer, take on new challenges, and perform at their best. Organizations can create a supportive workplace culture by:

- Encouraging work-life balance and well-being
- Providing opportunities for professional growth and development
- Recognizing and rewarding performance and achievements
- Celebrating diversity and promoting inclusion

- Creating a sense of community and belonging
- Providing access to resources such as employee assistance programs, mental health services, and wellness programs
- Creating a safe and respectful workplace that is free from harassment and discrimination

Promoting Work-Life Balance

Work-life balance is essential for women to be successful in the workplace. Women often have to juggle multiple roles, including caregiver, parent, and employee, and balancing these roles can be challenging. Organizations can promote work-life balance by:

- Offering flexible work arrangements such as telecommuting, job sharing, and flexible schedules
- Providing paid time off for personal and family needs
- Providing access to child care and elder care services
- Encouraging employees to take breaks and recharge
- Encouraging a culture of self-care and well-being

Closing the Gender Pay Gap

The gender pay gap is a significant barrier to women's empowerment in the workplace. Despite progress made over the years, women still earn less than men, and the gap is even wider for women of color. Organizations can close the gender pay gap by:

- o Conducting regular gender pay equity analyses and taking corrective actions
- o Ensuring that job descriptions and salary structures are gender-neutral
- o Implementing transparent pay practices
- o Offering salary negotiation training and resources to women
- o Providing equal pay for equal work regardless of gender or other characteristics

Encouraging Women's Leadership Development

Encouraging women's leadership development is essential for achieving gender parity in the workplace.

Organizations can provide leadership development opportunities for women by:

> Offering leadership training and mentoring programs
> Providing opportunities to lead projects and initiatives
> Encouraging women to participate in industry associations and professional organizations
> Encouraging women to take on leadership roles on boards and committees
> Providing sponsorship and advocacy for women's advancement

Conclusion

Empowering women in the workplace is critical for achieving gender parity and advancing sustainable economic growth. Organizations can take several steps to empower women, including promoting gender diversity, addressing bias and stereotypes, creating a supportive workplace culture, promoting work-life balance, closing the gender pay gap, and encouraging women's leadership development. These strategies not only benefit women but also benefit organizations by increasing innovation, productivity, and profitability.

Achieving gender parity in the workplace is a journey, and organizations that are committed to this goal will reap the rewards of a diverse and inclusive workforce that drives success and growth.

Increasing Women's Political Participation and Representation

Introduction

The world today is witnessing a significant shift in the role of women in society, with women increasingly taking up leadership roles in various fields. However, when it comes to politics, women are still underrepresented. Even in countries that have made significant strides in gender equality, women remain a minority in political leadership positions. This article will discuss the importance of empowering women in politics, the barriers that women face in political participation, and strategies for increasing women's political representation.

Importance of Empowering Women in Politics

There are several reasons why it is essential to empower women in politics. Firstly, women's participation in politics is crucial for achieving gender equality. When women have a seat at the table, they can advocate for policies that benefit women and girls, including policies related to reproductive rights, equal pay, and gender-based violence. Secondly, women's participation in politics is essential for the overall health of democracy. When women are not adequately represented, the perspectives and experiences of half of the population are not considered, leading to policies that do not reflect the needs and desires of the entire population. Finally, when women participate in politics, it can inspire other women and girls to get involved, creating a cycle of increased participation and representation.

Barriers to Women's Political Participation

Despite the importance of women's participation in politics, there are several barriers that prevent women from getting involved. These barriers include:

1. Patriarchal attitudes and stereotypes: Many societies still hold patriarchal attitudes and beliefs that women should not be involved in politics. These attitudes can lead

to discrimination and bias against women who seek political office.

2. Lack of access to education and resources: In many countries, women have limited access to education and resources, which can prevent them from developing the skills and knowledge necessary to participate in politics.

3. Gender-based violence and harassment: Women who seek political office may face gender-based violence and harassment, which can deter them from running for office or speaking out on important issues.

4. Lack of support from political parties: Political parties may be reluctant to nominate women for office, leading to a lack of representation in elected positions.

Strategies for Increasing Women's Political Representation

There are several strategies for increasing women's political representation, including:

1. Quotas: Quotas are a policy tool that can be used to increase the representation of women in politics. Quotas can take many

forms, including legal requirements for a certain percentage of women on candidate lists or reserved seats for women in parliament. Quotas have been successful in increasing women's political representation in countries such as Norway, France, and Rwanda.

2. Education and training: Education and training programs can provide women with the skills and knowledge necessary to participate in politics effectively. These programs can include training in public speaking, campaigning, and leadership.

3. Political parties' internal policies: Political parties can adopt internal policies that support the nomination and election of women. These policies can include gender quotas for candidate lists or the adoption of a code of conduct to address gender-based violence and harassment.

4. Outreach and engagement: Political parties and civil society organizations can engage in outreach efforts to encourage women to participate in politics. These efforts can include targeted campaigns to recruit women candidates or the provision of resources to support women's campaigns.

Conclusion

Empowering women in politics is essential for achieving gender equality and promoting democratic governance. Despite the barriers that women face, there are several strategies that can be used to increase women's political representation. Quotas, education and training, political parties' internal policies, and outreach and engagement efforts can all contribute to increasing the number of women in elected positions. By taking these steps, we can work towards a future where women have equal representation and influence in political decision-making.

Introduction

Women entrepreneurship has emerged as a powerful tool to promote gender equality and economic growth worldwide. According to a study by Global Entrepreneurship Monitor (GEM), women entrepreneurship rates have increased by 13% globally in recent years. However, there is still a huge gap in gender representation in entrepreneurship, and women face unique challenges such as lack of access to capital, networks, and business support services. To promote women entrepreneurship and gender equality, there is a need to empower women with the right tools, resources, and networks to start and grow successful and sustainable businesses.

Access to Capital

Access to capital is one of the biggest barriers to women's entrepreneurship.

Women-owned businesses receive only 2% of venture capital funding and 4% of small business loans. This lack of access to funding makes it difficult for women to start and grow their businesses. To address this issue, governments, NGOs, and private organizations are taking steps to increase access to capital for women entrepreneurs. Programs such as microfinance, crowdfunding, and angel investing are some of the ways in which women entrepreneurs can access capital. Additionally, governments can provide tax incentives and grants for women-owned businesses, and banks can offer preferential loan terms to women entrepreneurs.

Mentorship and Networking

Mentorship and networking are critical to the success of any entrepreneur, but it is even more important for women entrepreneurs who often face unique challenges. Mentors can provide guidance, advice, and support to women entrepreneurs and help them navigate the challenges of starting and growing a business. Networking can also help women entrepreneurs connect with other entrepreneurs, investors, and business leaders who can provide valuable insights and resources. To encourage mentorship and networking among women entrepreneurs, organizations can establish mentorship programs, organize networking events, and create online communities where women entrepreneurs can connect and collaborate.

Business Support Services

Access to business support services such as legal, accounting, and marketing can be a challenge for women entrepreneurs. Many women lack the resources and networks to access these services, which can be crucial to the success of their businesses. To address this issue, governments, NGOs, and private organizations can provide training and support to women entrepreneurs to help them access these services. For example, organizations can offer legal clinics, accounting workshops, and marketing boot camps to help women entrepreneurs build their skills and knowledge.

Work-Life Balance

Work-life balance is a challenge for all entrepreneurs, but it is especially difficult for women entrepreneurs who often juggle multiple roles as caregivers and business owners. To address this issue, organizations can provide flexible work arrangements such as telecommuting and job sharing, and offer support services such as childcare and eldercare. Additionally, governments can provide tax incentives and subsidies for businesses that offer family-friendly policies such as paid parental leave and flexible work arrangements.

Access to Markets

Access to markets is another challenge that women entrepreneurs face. Women-owned businesses often struggle to enter and compete in male-dominated markets. To address this issue, organizations can provide training and support to women entrepreneurs to help them develop their marketing and sales skills. Additionally, governments can provide incentives for businesses that source from women-owned businesses and provide preferential treatment to women-owned businesses in government procurement processes.

Innovation and Technology

Innovation and technology are key drivers of economic growth, and women entrepreneurs need to be at the forefront of these developments. However, women entrepreneurs often lack access to the latest technologies and innovation networks, which can limit their ability to compete in the marketplace. To address this issue, organizations can provide training and support to women entrepreneurs to help them develop their technology and innovation skills. Additionally, governments can provide tax incentives and grants for women-owned businesses that invest in innovation and technology, and encourage partnerships between women-owned businesses and technology companies.

Cultural and Social Barriers

Cultural and social barriers are often overlooked but can have a significant impact on women's entrepreneurship. In many cultures, women are expected to prioritize their family and household responsibilities over their careers. Additionally, women often face discrimination and bias in male-dominated industries. To address these barriers, organizations can work to change cultural and social norms that limit women's participation in entrepreneurship. This can include campaigns that promote the benefits of women's entrepreneurship, education programs that challenge gender stereotypes, and initiatives that encourage women's participation in male-dominated industries.

Advocacy and Policy Reform

Advocacy and policy reform are essential for creating an enabling environment for women's entrepreneurship. Governments and international organizations can advocate for policies that promote gender equality and support women's entrepreneurship. This can include policies that address the gender pay gap, provide access to affordable childcare, and support women's access to education and training. Additionally, governments can work to create an enabling regulatory environment for women's entrepreneurship, by removing legal and regulatory barriers and providing incentives for businesses that support gender equality.

Conclusion

Empowering women in entrepreneurship is not only a matter of social justice but also a key driver of economic growth and innovation. By providing women entrepreneurs with the right tools, resources, and networks, we can create a more inclusive and prosperous society. Governments, NGOs, and private organizations all have a role to play in promoting women's entrepreneurship, and by working together, we can build a world where women have the opportunity to start and grow successful and sustainable businesses.

Chapter 9. Women's Empowerment and Technology
Harnessing the Power of Digital Tools to Advance Gender Equality

Introduction

Women's empowerment is a crucial factor in achieving gender equality and social justice. It involves providing women with the necessary skills, knowledge, and resources to take control of their lives and make informed decisions. In recent years, technology has emerged as a powerful tool in the fight for women's empowerment, opening up new opportunities and creating new avenues for growth and development.

Technology has enabled women to connect with one another, access information, and engage in activities that were previously out of reach. The use of digital tools has created new opportunities for women to develop their skills, build their networks, and advance their careers. This article explores the ways in which technology is being used to advance women's empowerment and promote gender equality.

Access to Information

One of the most significant barriers to women's empowerment is the lack of access to information. In many parts of the world, women are not provided with the same educational opportunities as men, leaving them without the knowledge and skills necessary to succeed in their personal and professional lives.

The internet has the potential to change this, providing women with access to a wealth of information and resources that were previously unavailable. With the click of a button, women can now access online courses, tutorials, and educational materials that can help them develop new skills and gain knowledge in a variety of fields.

The internet has also opened up new avenues for communication, allowing women to connect with one another and share information and experiences. Social media platforms like Facebook and Twitter have become powerful tools for building communities of women who can support and empower one another.

Economic Empowerment

Another critical aspect of women's empowerment is economic independence. When women have the resources and skills necessary to support themselves and their families, they are better able to make informed decisions about their lives and futures.

Technology has created new opportunities for women to participate in the economy and achieve financial independence. Online marketplaces like Etsy and eBay allow women to sell their products and services to a global audience, while remote work opportunities and online job boards make it easier for women to find work that fits their schedules and skills.

In addition to providing women with economic opportunities, technology has also made it easier for women to manage their finances and investments. Mobile banking apps and online investment platforms allow women to take control of their financial futures, without the need for traditional brick-and-mortar banking services.

Education and Skills Development

Access to education and training is another critical factor in women's empowerment. By developing new skills and knowledge, women can expand their opportunities and pursue their goals more effectively.

Technology has made it easier for women to access educational opportunities and develop new skills. Online learning platforms like Coursera and Udemy provide access to a range of courses and tutorials, allowing women to learn at their own pace and on their own schedule.

Technology has also created new opportunities for skills development, particularly in fields that are traditionally male-dominated. Coding boot camps and online coding courses are opening up new opportunities for women to pursue careers in technology and other fields that require technical skills.

Health and Well-Being

Women's health and well-being are critical factors in their overall empowerment. Unfortunately, women often face significant barriers to accessing healthcare and other essential services, particularly in developing countries.

Technology has the potential to change this, providing women with access to a range of health and wellness resources. Mobile health apps and telemedicine platforms allow women to connect with healthcare providers and receive medical advice and treatment from the comfort of their own homes.

Technology is also being used to provide women with access to essential services like clean water and sanitation. In many parts of the world, women are responsible for collecting water and caring for their families' health and well-being. Access to clean water and sanitation can reduce the burden on women and improve their health outcomes, allowing them to pursue other opportunities.

Safety and Security

One of the most significant barriers to women's empowerment is the fear of violence and harassment. Women are often subject to discrimination, harassment, and violence, both in their personal and professional lives.

Technology can play a vital role in promoting women's safety and security. Mobile apps like Circle of 6 and bSafe allow women to quickly and discreetly alert their friends and family if they feel unsafe or need help. Social media platforms like Twitter and Facebook have also become powerful tools for raising awareness about issues related to women's safety and security.

In addition to promoting women's safety, technology can also be used to hold perpetrators of violence and harassment accountable. Social media campaigns like #MeToo have highlighted the prevalence of sexual harassment and assault, while online reporting systems and hotlines allow women to report incidents of violence and harassment safely and anonymously.

Conclusion

Technology has the potential to be a powerful tool in advancing women's empowerment and promoting gender equality. By providing women with access to information, economic opportunities, education and skills development, health and well-being resources, and safety and security measures, technology can help women overcome the barriers that have traditionally held them back.

However, it is important to recognize that technology alone is not enough. To truly achieve gender equality and women's empowerment, we must also work to address the underlying social, cultural, and economic factors that contribute to gender inequality.

By harnessing the power of technology in combination with other strategies, we can create a more equitable and just society for women around the world. As we continue to innovate and develop new digital tools, we must remain focused on the goal of empowering women and promoting gender equality, to ensure that everyone has the opportunity to reach their full potential.

Chapter 10. The Role of Men in Women's Empowerment
Allies, Advocates, and Agents of Change

Introduction

The journey towards gender equality is a long and challenging one. While significant progress has been made in recent years, women still face systemic barriers in various aspects of their lives. Empowering women and girls is not just a matter of fairness and justice; it is a critical driver for sustainable development and economic growth. However, women cannot achieve gender equality alone. Men must also play a crucial role as allies, advocates, and agents of change in the pursuit of women's empowerment.

Allyship: Standing in Solidarity with Women

The first step towards men's engagement in women's empowerment is becoming an ally. Allyship involves standing in solidarity with women and recognizing that gender equality is not just a women's issue but a human issue. Men can start by educating themselves on issues such as the gender pay gap, violence against women, and the lack of women's representation in leadership positions. By understanding these issues, men can better recognize their privilege and how it contributes to the marginalization of women.

Moreover, men can become active listeners and amplify women's voices by acknowledging their experiences and perspectives. This can be done by engaging in conversations, sharing resources, and providing support. It is essential to note that allyship is not a one-time event; it is a lifelong commitment to promoting gender equality and actively challenging sexism and misogyny.

Advocacy: Using Privilege to Create Change

As allies, men can leverage their privilege and position to advocate for gender equality. This involves using their platform to amplify women's voices and advocate for policies and practices that promote gender equality. Men can use their influence to challenge gender stereotypes and promote inclusive behaviors and attitudes.

For example, men in leadership positions can prioritize gender diversity and inclusion in their hiring and promotion decisions. They can advocate for policies that support women's participation in the workforce, such as paid parental leave, flexible work arrangements, and equal pay. Furthermore, men can challenge toxic masculinity and promote healthy relationships by modeling respectful and empathetic behavior towards women and encouraging other men to do the same.

Agent of Change: Taking Action Towards Women's Empowerment

To become true agents of change, men must take action towards women's empowerment. This involves actively working to dismantle the systemic barriers that prevent women from reaching their full potential. Men can work towards creating a more inclusive and equitable society by advocating for policy changes, supporting women-led initiatives, and challenging sexist attitudes and behaviors.

Moreover, men can actively seek out opportunities to support women in their personal and professional development. This can include mentoring, sponsoring, and providing access to networks and resources. By doing so, men can help address the lack of women's representation in leadership positions and support women's career advancement.

Conclusion

Men must play a critical role in women's empowerment. As allies, advocates, and agents of change, men can use their privilege and position to promote gender equality and challenge sexism and misogyny. It is essential to recognize that gender equality is not just a women's issue but a human issue. Men's engagement in women's empowerment is not just a matter of fairness and justice, but it is also a critical driver for sustainable development and economic growth. Together, men and women can create a more inclusive and equitable society where everyone has the opportunity to reach their full potential.

Chapter 11. Empowering Women Globally
Best Practices and Lessons Learned from Around the World

Introduction

Women's empowerment is critical for the achievement of sustainable development goals, gender equality, and social progress worldwide. Unfortunately, despite considerable progress in recent years, women still face significant challenges to access education, employment opportunities, and leadership roles. However, many countries have developed successful policies, programs, and initiatives that have helped to promote women's empowerment and gender equality. In this article, we will explore some of the best practices and lessons learned from around the world in empowering women and promoting gender equality.

Political Representation

Political representation is critical for promoting women's empowerment and gender equality. Women's representation in political institutions helps to ensure that women's voices are heard, their interests are taken into account, and policies are designed to address their specific needs. Many countries have implemented policies to increase women's representation in political institutions, such as quotas, reserved seats, and gender parity laws.

For example, Rwanda has the highest percentage of women in parliament in the world, with women holding 64% of seats in the lower house. This is largely due to the country's quota system, which requires that at least 30% of parliamentary seats be reserved for women. Other countries that have implemented similar policies include Bolivia, Colombia, Costa Rica, Ecuador, France, and Norway.

Education and Training

Access to education and training is critical for women's empowerment and economic development. Education provides women with the knowledge, skills, and resources they need to participate fully in society and achieve their potential. In many countries, however, women still face significant barriers to accessing education, such as poverty, cultural norms, and gender-based violence.

To overcome these barriers, many countries have implemented policies and programs to promote girls' education and training. For example, the Malala Fund, founded by Nobel Prize winner Malala Yousafzai, works to ensure that all girls have access to 12 years of free, safe, and quality education. The organization provides grants, advocacy, and training to support girls' education in countries like Pakistan, Nigeria, and Afghanistan.

Economic Empowerment

Economic empowerment is critical for women's autonomy, well-being, and social status. Women's economic participation not only benefits individuals and families but also contributes to the overall economic growth and development of societies. However, women still face significant barriers to economic empowerment, such as unequal pay, limited access to credit and markets, and gender-based discrimination.

To overcome these barriers, many countries have implemented policies and programs to promote women's economic empowerment.

For example, the Women Entrepreneurs Finance Initiative (We-Fi), launched by the World Bank, aims to support women entrepreneurs in developing countries by providing financing, training, and mentorship. The initiative has already mobilized over $1.6 billion in financing and supported more than 130,000 women entrepreneurs.

Health and Well-being

Access to health care and services is critical for women's empowerment and well-being. Women's health is not only a matter of human rights but also a driver of social and economic progress. Unfortunately, many women still face significant barriers to accessing health care and services, such as lack of resources, gender-based violence, and cultural norms.

To overcome these barriers, many countries have implemented policies and programs to promote women's health and well-being. For example, the Maternal and Child Survival Program (MCSP), launched by the United States Agency for International Development (USAID), aims to improve the health of women and children in developing countries by providing training, technical assistance, and support to health systems. The program has already helped to improve maternal and child health outcomes in countries like Ethiopia, India, and Nigeria.

Women's Rights and Empowerment

Women's empowerment and gender equality cannot be achieved without the protection and promotion of women's rights. Women's rights include the right to equality, non-discrimination, freedom from violence and exploitation, and the right to participate in political, economic, and social life on an equal basis with men. Unfortunately, many women still face significant violations of their rights, including gender-based violence, forced marriage, and human trafficking.

To overcome these challenges, many countries have implemented policies and programs to promote women's rights and empowerment. For example, the United Nations Women's Empowerment Principles (WEPs) provide a framework for businesses to promote gender equality and women's empowerment in the workplace, marketplace, and community. The WEPs have been adopted by more than 4,000 companies worldwide and have helped to promote women's leadership, equal pay, and safe working conditions.

Partnerships and Collaboration

Empowering women and promoting gender equality requires the collaboration and partnership of various stakeholders, including governments, civil society, private sector, and international organizations. By working together, these stakeholders can share resources, expertise, and best practices to promote women's empowerment and gender equality.

For example, the United Nations Development Programme (UNDP) has partnered with the private sector to promote women's economic empowerment in developing countries. The Gender Equality Seal Certification Programme helps companies to adopt gender-responsive policies and practices and provides training and support to promote women's leadership and participation in the workplace.

Conclusion

Empowering women and promoting gender equality is critical for the achievement of sustainable development goals, social progress, and human rights worldwide. Many countries have developed successful policies, programs, and initiatives to promote women's empowerment and gender equality. These best practices and lessons learned can serve as a guide for other countries and stakeholders to promote women's empowerment and gender equality. By working together, we can create a world where women have equal opportunities, rights, and dignity.

"Empowered Women, Empowered World" explores the critical topic of women's empowerment. The book comprises eleven insightful chapters that offer a comprehensive understanding of women's empowerment, including its definition, challenges, and opportunities. The chapters cover a range of topics such as the power of education in empowering women, breaking down health barriers for women, and strategies for achieving gender parity and advancement in the workplace. The book also explores the intersection of race, gender, and empowerment, and highlights the experiences of women of color. It delves into the role of men in women's empowerment, and examines the best practices and lessons learned from empowering women globally. This book is a valuable resource for anyone interested in promoting gender equality and creating an empowered world for women.

ABOUT THE AUTHOR

Mr. C. P. Kumar is a retired Scientist 'G' from the National Institute of Hydrology, Roorkee, Uttarakhand, India. With a wealth of experience in his field, he has also been practicing alternative healing therapies for several years. He is skilled in Reiki Healing and Chakra Balancing with Pendulum Dowsing, and offers holistic therapy through Emotional Freedom Technique (EFT) for emotional issues. You can email Mr. Kumar at cpkumar@yahoo.com and also visit his Reiki blog at https://reiki-roorkee.blogspot.com/ for more information.